CHANDA WEBB

THE CONFIDENT CLOSER

Helping New Agents Start With Heart–And Close With Confidence

OAK & WEBB
— PRESS —

Contents

Acknowledgments

This book is the result of years of learning, listening, and leaning into growth—both professionally and personally.

To **John Sass**, my broker owner—thank you for leading with integrity and excellence. Your consistency and presence over the years have set the standard for what it means to operate with professionalism and adaptability in this ever-changing industry.

To **Dennis DiSabato**, my broker-manager—your check-ins, your patience, and your guidance made a tremendous impact on how I approach this business. Your words, "How's business going?" were never just a question—they were a reminder to stay intentional and accountable.

To **Susan Mazetta** and **Jill Savva**—thank you for your steady leadership, insight, and support. The culture of our office and the confidence I've developed wouldn't be what they are without your contribution and presence.

You all have been in this business long before algorithms, apps, and automation—and your old-school wisdom, blended with modern adaptability, has been a masterclass in longevity and excellence. Your commitment to showing up with positivity and professionalism every day continues to inspire me.

To my **fellow agents and and the entire team at the Century 21 Cedarcrest Office**—thank you for sharing the journey. From role-playing scripts to celebrating closings, your teamwork, encouragement, and shared wisdom have shaped me more than you know. I've grown alongside you, and I'm proud to be part of such a dedicated and supportive team.

To my **clients**—thank you for trusting me. Every conversation, showing, and closing has been more than business—it's been personal. You've helped me grow in ways I could never predict.

To my **family and friends**—your encouragement has been the quiet strength behind everything I do. Thank you for believing in me when I was still learning to believe in myself.

And to the **new agents reading this**:

I wrote this for you. Let this be your reminder that you don't need to have all the answers—you just need the courage to ask the right questions, serve with integrity, and show up even when you're nervous.

This book is a thank you to everyone who helped me to become a **Confident Closer.**

With deep gratitude,

Chanda

1

Helping People, Finding People

In my previous roles—whether in social services, workforce development, advisement, or teaching—people usually came to me with a problem they needed help solving. I was the guide, the support system, and the steady presence they could lean on when the next step felt uncertain. I was used to that. I did this all of my adult life. Those years taught me patience, resilience, and how to meet people where they are. I didn't realize it then, but those very skills would become the backbone of everything I later did in real estate.

In 2015, something shifted in my life.

That year, my daughter finished her undergraduate degree and then went overseas for graduate school. Just like that, she walked across the stage in June, and by September, she was on a plane to Europe. As I prepared her for her next chapter, I started thinking hard about my own. For the first time in years, I had space to ask myself: *What's next for me?*

It was both unsettling and exciting to realize I finally had to answer that question for myself.

At the time, I was working as a Transfer Advisor for a community college, guiding students through their own big transitions—helping them move from two-year schools to four-year universities. I even considered going back to finish a master's degree in Psychology myself. I had six credits completed already, but the thought of taking on student loans just didn't sit right with me. I thought about counseling. I thought about teaching full-time. I even thought about staying put and climbing higher where I was.

But none of it felt like the new chapter I was looking for. More than that, I began to feel that while I still wanted to help people—but in a way that freed me from the traditional structures I had always worked under. I was ready for a change, even if I didn't yet know what it was. I spent weeks wondering what kind of career could give me both a new challenge and the chance to keep working closely with people.

That search led me somewhere I had not expected—real estate. A field I knew little about, but one I couldn't stop being curious about.

As I grew more interested in taking that route, I noticed something that changed the way I thought about my people skills. In social services, people usually came to me when they needed help or support. In fact, every client I worked with was already in a place of need, and I was there to guide them towards resources or opportunities.

Real estate turned that around. Instead of waiting for people to find me, I had to go out and find them. I had to earn their trust before I could even begin to help. And honestly, for a while, I didn't know how to carry my "helping profession" skills into a space where I was competing for business instead of simply supporting needs.

The expectations felt sky-high, and it took time to realize that what I already had still mattered — it just needed a different approach. While still working full-time as a Transfer Advisor, I enrolled in the Montclair School of Real Estate. My days were packed — I spent hours helping students prepare for their next step in college, then headed straight to evening classes where I was preparing for my own next steps. After weeks of late nights and long commutes, I passed the course exam and then the state exam. Holding that license in my hand felt like both relief and responsibility.

But passing the test was only the beginning. I kept working full-time at the college even as I started building my real estate business. I began telling people at work that I was a new agent. I called friends and family to let them know I was in real estate. I even used personal days from work to attend training sessions and workshops so I could get a better handle on the business. Evenings and weekends became my time to experiment — trying small things, introducing myself, and slowly figuring out how to show up as an agent while still balancing my full-time job.

My first listing came from a woman I used to see almost every day.

She was a crossing guard in my town, and I passed her regularly on my way to catch the train. For a while, I would just nod or smile, but one day, I worked up the courage to actually say something.

While standing at the crosswalk, waiting for the light to change, I handed her my card. I didn't even ask her name.

I was so focused on doing something—on putting myself out there—that just giving out my card felt like a win.

At the time, nothing came of it. She thanked me and we went about our days.

But a few weeks later, she told me something I'll never forget: she and her husband had tried to sell their house a few years earlier, and the listing had expired and that they gave up trying. She said she'd let me know if they ever decided to try again.

Not long after that, she did. She asked me, to help her sell her house. That listing meant everything to me — it wasn't just my first transaction, it was the first time I realized that showing up, even in the smallest ways, really matters. I didn't have a polished pitch. I didn't ask for her contact information. I just took a step, and that step turned into trust.

I listed and sold their home, and today, she's not just a past client— she's a friend who has even sent me referrals. That first "yes" taught me something I still carry: boldness doesn't always feel bold. Sometimes, it looks like handing someone a card while waiting at a crosswalk.

The Lesson

Here's what I learned: while the environment was different, the people were still people.

The skills I had, the listening, the empathy, the emotional intelligence—were not lost in translation.

They just needed to be restructured and re-targeted. You may come into real estate with transferable skills that don't seem to "fit" at first, but they will, once you realize this: real estate is not just about selling homes—it's about serving people.

Whether you come from education, healthcare, retail, or administration, there's a place for your past in your future success as an agent. You don't have to unlearn who you are to be successful in real estate. You just have to re-frame it.

Taking It Further

If you've ever helped someone solve a problem, If you've ever coached, taught, listened, encouraged, or shown up for someone, Then you already have the raw ingredients to succeed here.

What changes is how those skills are activated. In social services, people came to me. In real estate, I had to go to them.

But the core stayed the same: people still needed someone they could trust. They just didn't always know it yet.

That's where your background becomes a secret strength—not a liability.

Whether you were the "go-to" person in your 9-5 job or the quiet encourager in your friend group, you already know how to show up. Now, you get to learn how to show up differently—before the contract, before the pitch, and before they even know they need you.

So, ask yourself:

- What do people naturally come to me for?
- What kind of support am I good at giving?
- Where in my past have, I helped someone move from stuck to ready?

Real estate is full of scripts—but connection can't be scripted. Start with what's true about you.

For me, that meant looking back at every job I'd held and asking: beyond the job description, what did I really do well? That was when I realized I wasn't just an employee with a title — I was much more than that. I was leading, coaching, teaching, listening, persuading, encouraging. I was solving problem in creative ways. I was a teacher, a job coach, a job developer, an advisor, a counselor. At the heart of it, I knew how to help people move from A to B. And that realization gave me the confidence to keep moving forward in real estate.

What I Know Now

Real estate challenged me in ways I didn't expect—but it also revealed strengths I didn't know I had. Coming from social services, I thought I was leaving behind both my purpose and my steady paycheck. What I discovered is that real estate has purpose, too—deep purpose. People don't just need agents who understand contracts. They need someone who sees them, supports them, and helps them step into one of life's biggest transitions with confidence.

That's not just a sale. That's service.

Looking back, I see now that this work still allows me to coach, teach, encourage, and problem-solve— and to keep learning.

I'm thankful for the guidance of my brokers and mentors who showed me that this profession is both an opportunity *and* a responsibility. They modeled steadiness, coaching ability, and integrity—the things that build a reputation beyond the marketing.

Real estate is a business. But it's also a people business. And if you love people, and you're willing to grow, there's room here for you.

I didn't have to leave my calling behind to be in this field. I just had to learn how to carry it differently. And now, I get to bring all of who I am into the homes and lives of the people I serve.

That's what makes this work worth it.

2

The Walk-Up Strategy

When I began my real estate career. I didn't have a car—a detail I used to be hesitant to share, but now I see it as a strength. While I was in real estate school—taking classes in the evenings after work—I knew in the back of my mind that I needed a car. But I wasn't going to let that stop me.

At the time, I took the train to work every day, and the fare was inexpensive enough to make it manageable. I even took the train to class. My focus was simple: pass the state exam, get started, and sell homes so I could afford a car.

I didn't hesitate once I had my license. I was upfront with brokers about my situation. Not having a car wasn't ideal, but it wasn't a deal-breaker for me—or for the people who were willing to give me a chance.

I also had an audience right in front of me—people I saw every day at my 9–5 job. I let them know I was a new agent starting my real estate business, and they were encouraging. Looking back,

I realize I didn't follow up as well as I could have, but I still knew I had easy access to potential clients. Sure enough, about a year later, one of my former co-workers bought a house through me. It reminded me that the seeds you plant now can bloom much later. Between train rides to my 9-5, evening classes, and those first neighborhood walks, I was learning on the fly what prospecting really meant.

I couldn't drive around and scout neighborhoods like other agents. So, I walked— Literally.

But I didn't start by knocking on doors. That felt a little too direct and overwhelming for me at the time. Instead, I approached people who were already outside—on their porches, walking their dogs, mowing the lawn, or heading to work. I recall how I would have my card ready in my pocket or my hand, ready to whip it out as soon as I saw someone on their lawn or standing still.

Although it may seemed a little forward in the beginning, it helped me break the ice, build visibility, and gain a little more confidence with every walk. I kept it simple and respectful.

I would say something like, *"Hi, I'm a local real estate agent and I'm walking the neighborhood today. I just wanted to introduce myself."* Then I'd hand them my card. That's it.

I didn't ask for phone numbers or emails at first. I didn't try to schedule an appointment right then and there. In fact, I wasn't even sure what the next step should be. I was nervous and didn't want to come across as pushy. I was just happy to hand over a card, provide a smile, and moved on.

But something surprising happened: people started calling me. Others saw me more than once and eventually approached me.

Another one of those early walk-ups turned into a real client. *This wasn't the crossing guard; this was a different neighbor.* She was getting into her car one morning, and I started walking fast to catch her before she got in. I gave her my card, told her that I lived in the neighborhood, and said if she had any questions she could call me.

A week or two later, she surprised me by flagging me down: "My husband and I are thinking about selling our house—what should we do?" My heart raced, and the first thing that came out of my mouth—and probably the best thing—was telling her, "I can stop by later and we can talk." We agreed. I had no idea what I would say, but I was ready to listen.

I remember sitting at their kitchen table, trying to "sell" myself as their agent—completely forgetting that they had already chosen me. I could have lost that listing, because I kept saying "if you decide to choose me," until she reminded me, that they wanted me to sell the property.

That moment taught me something important: the connection was already made. I didn't need to oversell. I just needed to be present.

The Lesson

You don't need to be perfect to get started. I didn't have a car, a script, or a system, I had my courage and my card.

That may not be a long-term strategy, but for me, it was a powerful beginning. You need presence, consistency, and a willingness to speak to people. Your first connections might feel clumsy, but they matter—and they can lead to real business.

Now, let me be clear: I don't recommend making business cards your entire strategy. Relying on people to call you back is risky, and you miss opportunities to stay in touch. But if you're new, nervous, or working with limited resources, it's a place to start.

Taking It Further

Starting small doesn't mean thinking small. That walk-up strategy wasn't just about handing out cards—it was about choosing to *show up*, even when you didn't feel ready, equipped, or impressive.

And that's something every agent—new or seasoned—needs to remember: You don't need the perfect setup to make a real connection. You just need to show up as someone who's *real*.

When you walk a neighborhood, you're not just looking for business. You're building trust with people who live there. You're planting seeds. You're becoming a familiar face in an environment crowded with messages and marketing. Most people aren't going to invite you to list their home after a single hello. But they *will* remember how you made them feel. Were you friendly, or pushy?

Did you seem interested in the person—or just the potential sale? If you're walking up to someone, the close isn't always for the contract—it might be for the *conversation*, the *connection*, or the *callback later*. Confident Closers understand that trust is built in layers. Every step forward counts.

Here are a few mindset shifts to keep with you as you walk: **You're not bothering people—you're becoming part of the neighborhood rhythm. You're not "selling yourself"—you're giving people a chance to know you. You're not waiting for a perfect moment—you're creating momentum.**

If you stay consistent and kind, people will start to see you as their "go-to," even before they realize they need you.

What I Know Now

Not having a car didn't hold me back. It revealed a strength I might have never uncovered otherwise: the power of being *present and visible*.

What I know now is this—real estate isn't about waiting until you have it all together. It's about starting with what you do have and using it well. People don't hire you because you're flashy. They hire you because you're real. Because you showed up. Because you kept showing up.

In a world crowded with ads, and automation, people still notice the human moments —the smile, the hello, the familiar face that shows up more than once. That is something money can't buy.

And if you're just starting out—or starting over—you don't need perfect tools to earn someone's trust. You need heart. You need consistency. And you need the courage to put yourself in motion.

I'm grateful that I learned that early, and I'm even more grateful that I had people in my office who didn't judge how I started. They respected the work—and they reminded me that *how* you begin doesn't limit where you can go. This business will meet you where you are. But only if you're willing to step forward— again and again.

3

Asking Without Feeling Awkward

When I was studying for my license, it never crossed my mind that talking to people in real estate would feel so awkward. In social services, conversations came naturally—I was helping people with needs they already knew they had. But in real estate, the conversations felt different. I wasn't sure how to shift from casual talk into business without sounding pushy.

Yes, you might meet a few people by helping at an open house, but a huge part of the work is learning how to approach people, start conversations, and ask the right questions.

In the beginning, I didn't realize how uncomfortable I would feel asking those questions. It wasn't that I didn't want to help; it was that I didn't know how to transition from casual conversation to business without feeling like I was pushing. I had to go from responding to the needs of people to discovering the needs of people.

In social services, you sometimes have to uncover hidden needs, but most of the time you already know why the person is there. They arrive with a referral, or the nature of the program makes their situation clear before they even sign their name. I rarely had to ask, and when I did, it was usually, "How can I help you?" or "What can I do for you?" because in those settings the need is stated. When I worked in a college setting as an advisor, for example, it was obvious that first-year students were there to choose classes. My job was to solve the problem or assist quickly and move on to the next person. In those roles I rarely had to break the ice—the ice was already broken. People came to me ready to talk.

When I became an agent, it felt awkward. People don't walk up to you just because you're wearing a pin with your name and company logo, and no one can tell you're a real estate agent just by looking at you. Suddenly I had to initiate contact instead of simply responding. There was no intake form, no automatic signal that someone needed my help. That shift forced me to rethink how I opened a conversation.

But over time, I came to understand something important: asking the right questions is a skill you must develop in this business. And that means you must talk.

When I first started approaching people, I avoided asking certain questions—not because I didn't care, but because I honestly didn't know how to transition into them naturally.

I would start with a warm, casual conversation—maybe ask their name or how long they lived in the neighborhood—but hit a wall. I didn't want it to feel like I was prying. Some of the question styles I had heard from other agents just didn't match my personality. They worked for them, but I needed to find an approach that felt more like me— something that allowed the conversation to flow without feeling forced.

I used to worry a lot about coming off as pushy. The last thing I wanted was to be that agent who talked too much, asked too soon, or made someone feel like they were just another name on a list.

That self-doubt made me second-guess myself in conversations, even when I had good intentions. Eventually, I had to shift my mindset. I began to see that I offer a service—and it's okay to ask questions that help people understand that.

Asking doesn't make you pushy. It makes you present, prepared, and professional. One moment that drove this home was when I finally stopped to speak with a woman I often saw in the mornings as she was taking her kids to school. She and her family lived just a few doors down from where I lived, and although I would wave to them regularly, I had never actually stopped to talk.

I hesitated, but finally said something like, "I'm sorry to bother you, I know you're busy, but I just wanted to give you my card to let you know I'm a local agent in the neighborhood." She smiled, thanked me for the card, and that was it. I didn't ask her name although I had seen her and her family several times.

At that time, I was so focused on not being pushy that I made myself sound almost apologetic—like I was doing something wrong by offering my card. Days passed before I saw her again, this time with her husband. We started talking and discovered more about each other: I had lived in the town for over twenty years, they had been there for more than thirty-five, and the wife had even attended the same high school that my daughter attended. They told me about the history of their home and their tenant upstairs. They also shared that they had talked many times about selling their home and, when the time came, wanted me to be their agent. And sure enough, not long after that conversation— the following spring—when they decided to sell, they asked me to represent them.

I was shocked. Honestly, I didn't expect it.

But I shouldn't have been surprised. This is what I signed up for. This is my career. I was needed—and thankfully, I had shown up, even if I felt a little awkward at the time.

The Lesson

That moment reminded me that even if I didn't say things perfectly, people could still feel my sincerity. I learned that I didn't have to downplay myself just to seem polite. Being helpful doesn't mean holding back.

I can show up with kindness and confidence, ask questions without fear, and trust in the value I bring to the table. Looking back, I know now that I was operating from a place of fear, not service. I had to make a mindset shift and remind myself why I was doing this.

I'm not just showing houses—I'm helping people make life-changing decisions. For a long time I assumed asking made me seem intrusive, but holding back only kept me from serving.

And honestly, I left a lot of conversations hanging—not because I didn't want the business, but because I was afraid of overstepping or making someone uncomfortable.

Asking the right questions isn't about pressuring. It's about showing up with purpose. When you ask with care, with clarity, and with confidence, people don't feel sold—they feel seen. That's when the conversation shifts. That's when trust begins.

Taking It Further

Looking back, I can't believe how awkward I once felt talking to people about real estate. Who feels awkward about going to work? Why should asking questions as an agent feel any different? After all, every business has to reach out.

The hesitation to ask comes from a good place: you want to be respectful, not a nuisance. But here's the truth — people rarely mind being asked when they sense your goal is to help, not to hustle.

When you approach with clarity and calm, you're not interrupting — you're guiding. You're reminding someone they have options and that you're a safe, steady person to explore those options with. Think of it this way: before someone even knows what they need, you're simply offering a bridge between curiosity and clarity, between "someday" and "maybe now." Sometimes the right question doesn't lead to an immediate answer — it opens the door to a relationship.

You don't need to script every line. What matters most is how you position yourself:

- as someone who listens
- as someone who helps navigate the unknown
- as someone who understands timing, readiness, and trust

Here's a simple shift in mindset: instead of asking, "How do I avoid sounding salesy?" ask, "How can I make this conversation about them?" When your questions are shaped by service, they land differently. They invite instead of intrude.

You're not trying to close a deal on the spot; you're building a conversation that moves someone closer to what they truly want — even if they haven't said it out loud yet.

What I Know Now

I came to understand that asking questions was never the problem. My fear of being pushy was. Real estate isn't about perfect timing or perfect wording—it's about showing up with sincerity. People don't remember whether you nailed the script; they remember whether you cared. When you ask with genuine curiosity, the conversation doesn't feel forced. It feels like trust.

4

Lead with People

In Chapter 3 I talked about finding my footing. This chapter is about using the skills I already had to lead with people first.

My years in education and social services gave me plenty of experience working with people. I helped individuals in finding jobs, access training, and navigate difficult life transitions. In those roles, people came to me. There was a system, a process, and a rhythm to the work.

Real estate was different. As an agent, you're not on a payroll. You're an independent contractor—an entrepreneur responsible for building and running your own business.

That didn't scare me. I've always known how to make things happen. But I quickly learned that while real estate has systems, scripts, and tools, none of them matter in the moment when it's just you, one other person, and an unexpected conversation. In that space, you lean on your instincts and your ability to connect.

At first, I didn't see it that way. When people made small-talk—
"The market's crazy, " or "Houses are selling fast, huh?'—I'd
nod or give a short answer. I didn't know how to turn those
comments into real conversations without sounding uneasy.

But I realized those weren't throwaway lines. They were open-
ings. People weren't just chatting—they were signaling curiosity or concern. They were testing whether I had something to
offer beyond a business card. That's when I learned: **connections comes before conversion**. People want to feel heard before
they'll trust you with something as major as buying or selling a
home.

Buyers and sellers may share the same market, but their motiva-
tions, emotions, and timelines are completely different. Some
are starting a new chapter, others are closing one. All of them
are in transition— and transition requires understanding.

I saw this firsthand at my open houses. Some visitors were
simply curious neighbors; some weren't ready to buy and just
wanted to look; others were trying to picture themselves as
future homeowners. I would collect names and numbers on the
sign-in sheet, but later discover that many phone numbers were
invalid or calls went unanswered. Those experiences taught me
that every open house is an opportunity to meet people where
they are in their journey, not just to collect leads.

In fact, the only real common ground between buyers and sellers
is change. Both are on the move, and their lives will look
different on the other side of the transaction. My job wasn't
to rush to the pitch—it was to meet them in that space of change

and help them feel steady in the process.

The Lesson

Here's what I learned: people don't expect you to have all the answers. They expect you to care. They expect you to listen, to ask questions that matter, and share insight that meets them where they are. That's where the relationship starts—not with a listing, but with a conversation.

Taking It Further

Yes, systems matter. Scripts matter. Market knowledge matters. But what earns trust isn't how fast you can recite stats—it's how well you can read the moment.

When someone says, *"The market's crazy,"* they're not always asking for data. They're testing to see if you're approachable, informed, and human. That's your cue—not to pitch, but to pause. Because when you lead with people, you naturally lead with the kind of presence that creates closings down the line.

Try shifting your mindset from:
   "What should I say next?" to *"What are they really asking me?"*

This doesn't mean you ignore the business — it means you build the bridge first.

Here are a few small habits that helped me:

- **Mirror the moment.** If they're casual, stay light. If they seem unsure, meet them with calm.
- **Ask before you inform.** Before sharing what you know, ask what they've heard or experienced.
- **Use shared language.** Don't correct their real estate lingo — reflect it back in a way that's easy to build on.
- **Respect the pause.** Not every opening leads to a pitch. Sometimes the win is simply being remembered as someone who didn't rush.

The confident closer isn't waiting to talk — they're waiting to understand. And when the time comes to list, buy, or refer, people will remember how you made them feel: heard, seen, and steady.

What I Know Now

What I know now is that I didn't merge my people skills with real estate right away. I thought I had to set aside what I already knew, follow the script, and everything would fall into place. But in doing that, I left a good part of myself out of the picture. It took time to realize that my natural strengths weren't separate from this work—they were the foundation of it. Leading with people isn't a tactic; it's how I do business now, and it's what makes every conversation feel more confident and natural.

5

What to Say When You Don't Know What to Say

There were times I didn't know what to say—and not just because I was nervous or new. Sometimes, I stayed quiet because I didn't feel like I knew the business well enough to carry the conversation.

Staying quiet isn't a bad thing. In fact, it's one of the best ways to truly listen and understand what someone needs. In my previous work, listening was a skill I relied on every day—it helped me read situations, pick up on unspoken concerns, and guide people toward solutions. But I quickly learned that in real estate, listening alone isn't enough. At some point, you have to speak. You have to respond, to ask, to guide the conversation forward. Listening opens the door, but talking—at the right time—helps you walk through it.

I thought I had to master the script before I could open my mouth. I attended the office training my broker offered, sat in the back, and take notes like I was back in school. But when I got out in the field—face-to-face with real people and real questions—I froze. It wasn't that I didn't know how to talk to people. I did. I just didn't want to fake it. I didn't want to fill the silence with fluff or say something just to sound like I knew what I was doing.

Looking back, I can see what was happening. I was so focused on saying the right thing that I forgot to focus on learning the real things. I was focused on remembering lines instead of learning the business. And I didn't want to say the wrong thing, so I sometimes didn't say anything at all.

There's one moment I'll never forget. I was meeting with a potential seller, and they asked a question I hadn't prepared for. It wasn't even a complicated one, but it threw me off because it wasn't in the script I had studied. I gave a vague, safe answer, and afterward, I beat myself up. I didn't lose the listing—but I lost an opportunity to really connect.

That's when I realized: real confidence doesn't come from sounding polished, it comes from being prepared. And that kind of preparation doesn't happen overnight. I had to get out there and learn the world of real estate—not just memorize phrases. I had to learn what buyers were afraid of, what sellers cared about, how deals moved, and what questions I needed to ask to truly help someone. That's when things started to click.

And even when I didn't know what to say, I learned that presence matters more than perfection. It's okay to pause. It's okay to say, "That's a great question—let me double-check so I can give you the most accurate answer." People respect honesty more than a rushed or robotic response.

25

One of the best pieces of advice I ever received came from my broker-manager: "Slow down."

When we practiced scripts in the office, I would talk a mile a minute—maybe out of nerves, maybe out of fear that the other person would cut me off. But that advice stuck with me. Slowing down helped me breathe, think, and listen. It reminded me that I belonged in the conversation. Even if I didn't have all the answers yet.

The Lesson

There were moments early in my journey where I stood in front of someone and literally drew a blank. My brain said, "Say something smart," and my mouth said... nothing. But I learned something important—being stuck for words doesn't mean you're unqualified. It just means you're human. What helped me was having a few go-to phrases, not to sound scripted, but to help me get started. The truth is you don't have to sound perfect—you just have to sound present. And when you lead with heart, "not hype", the right words start to come.

Taking It Further

Uncertainty doesn't mean you're unprepared—it means you're growing.

There will always be questions you don't expect. That's not a failure. That's the nature of a people-based business. Buyers, sellers, and even neighbors will throw things at you that aren't in the handbook—and that's okay.

Your job isn't to have a polished answer for every scenario.

Your job is to be present enough to respond with thought, curiosity, or follow-up when needed.

You don't lose trust when you pause. You lose it when you pretend.

Instead of fearing silence, learn to work with it:

- **Ask a follow-up:** "Can you tell me a little more about that?"
- **Be honest:** "I'd like to confirm that so I can give you the most accurate answer."
- **Guide the next step:** "There are a few ways that could go—want me to gather the details for you?"

These aren't filler lines. They're bridges—from pressure to partnership.

Here's the shift: Don't treat every conversation like a quiz. Treat it like a collaboration. Your role isn't to impress—it's to *inform*, *support*, and *guide*. And sometimes, that starts by admitting, "I'd like to look into that further for you."

You don't need to be perfect to be trusted. You just need to be honest, composed, and willing to keep learning.

What I know Now

Blank moments don't define you. They shape you. I used to think silence meant I wasn't ready. Now I see it as space — space to breathe, to listen, and to answer with more honesty than I could have in a rush.

6

Scripts That Sound Like You

In the beginning, I wasn't handed a binder full of scripts. The early focus was simple: get out there, talk to people, and build momentum as you learned in real time. And to be honest, that wasn't a bad approach. It forced me to engage.

But once I started to grow and observe how seasoned agents operated, I began to understand the power of using a well-structured script.

Let me be clear: I believe in scripts.

Scripts are not about sounding robotic or rehearsed—they're about having direction. They give you a foundation when your nerves take over, when conversations go off course, or when you're simply unsure what to say next. They're tools that offer rhythm, clarity, and confidence—if you know how to make them sound like you.

The truth is, some of the best agents I've met use scripts every single day. You just wouldn't know it. That's the beauty of it. They have practiced so much, internalized the structure, and blended in their personality so well that it comes out sounding natural—like a real conversation.

What stood out to me most wasn't just what they said, but how they showed up:

- They asked smart follow-up questions.
- They listened more than they talked.
- They weren't afraid to say, "I'm not sure, but I'll find out."
- They let silence do some of the work.

Watching them helped me realize something important: Scripts aren't supposed to replace your voice—they're meant to support it. For me, that meant asking questions that sounded like me. When I was walking neighborhoods and talking with homeowners—especially as I became less nervous—I liked to ask what had first attracted them to their home. What was their story in the beginning? I asked questions like these because I love a good story, and that made me feel comfortable. Usually, that's a question for a meeting with a seller, but I found it worked beautifully right there on a porch or out on the lawn. I also began to ask about their experience with their Realtor—what the person was like and what stood out about working with them. These weren't "script questions," but they opened doors. People didn't mind sharing, and their answers gave me valuable insight into how people think about buying and selling, long before they were ready to move.

A script is like a recipe—it gives you structure until the rhythm becomes second nature. Once you know it well, you can make small adjustments that make it sound natural and authentic to your voice.

I also had to learn to let go of the pressure to "say it perfectly." Early on, I would stumble through scripts because I was so focused on getting the words right.

But sounding confident isn't about perfect delivery—it's about honest delivery. And honest delivery starts with believing in what you're saying.

Taking It Further

The best scripts aren't written to be repeated word-for-word forever. They're written to give you footing while you learn the rhythm of real conversations. When you internalize a script, you're not just memorizing words—you're learning to guide a moment with confidence.

Practice Tip: Record yourself reading a script. Play it back and rewrite anything that doesn't sound like you. Then role-play with a colleague or friend until it feels conversational.

That's why delivery matters. Your tone, pacing, presence, and intention shape how your words land far more than the exact phrasing does.

Here's what happens when you *own* the script:

You stop reciting, and start responding.

You stop chasing approval, and start building connection.

You stop asking from a place of fear and start offering from a place of service.

Think of it like this: you wouldn't read a recipe out loud at the dinner table. But you might follow it in the kitchen until the meal becomes second nature. Scripts work the same way.

Use them as a launchpad—not a lifeline.

As you grow, adapt them. Put them in your own words. Add pauses. Emphasize what feels most natural to you. Practice aloud until it sounds like something you'd say on a Tuesday morning—not just what you memorized from a list.

Because that's what clients remember—not perfection, but presence. Not a polished pitch, but a conversation that feels genuine.

Scripts are just the starting line. The confident closer practices them, personalizes them, and uses them until they can guide a conversation without even thinking about the next line. That's when your attention shifts from "getting it right" to giving the person in front of you exactly what they need.

7

Keep Building Even After the Close

There's nothing like closing your first deal. The excitement. The celebration. The validation that you can do this.

But after one of my early closings, my broker told me something I'll never forget:

"Guess what? You're out of business. Go get more."

That statement wasn't discouraging—it was honest. It reminded me that in real estate, the close isn't the finish line. It's a checkpoint. Every time you close a deal, you're starting again. That mindset is what separates agents who thrive from those who get comfortable.

In a traditional job, the tasks are there whether you show up or not. There's structure, predictability, and someone else assigning the work. But in real estate, if you don't show up, the work doesn't get done. You are the business. You're the marketing department, the operations manager, and the customer service team all in one.

When I closed my first few deals, I felt great. But I also noticed how quickly the momentum could fade if I didn't keep moving. My broker's words echoed in my head every time I thought about taking it easy: "You're out of business. Go get more."

After my second closing, I started calling everyone I knew about the closing, I spent time sending emails, going through the my database, and sending post-cards to nearby homeowners. I was motivated.

I learned that you have to treat real estate like a business with daily habits. You can't just wait for leads or rely on yesterday's wins. I committed to:

- Attending weekly training—even when I was tired or felt like I already knew the topic.
- Calling past clients to check in, not just to ask for business.
- Keeping track of how many people I spoke to each day.
- Making it part of my routine to show up—even on days when I didn't have appointments.

There's a rhythm to this business. You prospect, you nurture, you serve, and you repeat. The challenge is not just to do it once, but to do it consistently. And the reward is that over time, people remember you. They refer you. They call you back—even when you gave them your card months ago while they were walking their dog.

Being in real estate means you're always building—relationships, systems, knowledge, and trust. So when you close a deal, celebrate it. But also, lace up your shoes. Because tomorrow, it's time to build again.

The Lesson

The closing table is not the finish line—it's a milestone. The agents who build solid businesses, they are the ones that keep showing up. I believe in checking in, celebrating wins, and staying connected long after the keys are handed over. Because your best marketing isn't a flyer—it's a former client who can say, 'She really cared.'

After one closing, I received a call from someone who was a friend of a client, and wanted to buy a home through me. I was so grateful that my former client thought about me and basically gave me a referral.

That kind of relationship doesn't happen by accident.

It's built through consistent, thoughtful follow-up—often in the middle of paperwork, deadlines, and plenty of emotions. But when you see a client's excitement at the closing table, it makes all of it worth it. Those moments remind you why the follow-up matters—because behind every transaction is a person who trusted you through one of life's biggest decisions. The goal isn't just to close the deal—it's to become the go-to person they trust for life.

Taking It Further

Every closing is proof that your systems, effort, and instincts worked. But it's also a reminder: momentum doesn't keep itself. You have to rebuild it—over and over again.

In this business, you're not just creating sales—you're creating cycles. And the most successful agents treat their follow-up like lead generation.

Here's the truth: people don't remember the flyer you mailed six months ago. They remember the unexpected check-in. They remember the agent who followed up without asking for anything. Long-term business isn't built in the busy, "hot" phase of a transaction—it's built in the quieter months that follow. The confident closer doesn't disappear after the deal is done.

They stay visible. They stay useful. They stay real.
Here are a few post-close rhythms that turn happy clients into loyal advocates:

- **Send** a 3-month "How's it going?" note with zero sales pitch.
- **Track** birthdays and home anniversaries—even if it's just on a spreadsheet.
- **Offer** unexpected value, like a trusted vendor contact or a quick home maintenance tip.
- **Make** your follow-up feel like friendship, not marketing.

And yes—it's okay to ask if they know someone who might be looking to buy or sell. But do it from a place of care, not as a transaction. People can tell when your call is about them versus when it's just about business. When you've built trust, that question feels like a natural part of the conversation—not a sales pitch.

You may not see an instant return—but trust compounds. And one day, they'll say, *"I know who to call."* Not because you asked, but because you never disappeared.

Remember: you're not just closing transactions—you're opening the door to lifelong relationships.

- Think of one past client you haven't reached out to in a while. What would it look like to reconnect—just to check in, no ask attached?

- Explore what a follow-up plan could look like for *you*. There are great companies, systems, and tools out there—just choose something that fits your style and schedule.

- Brainstorm 3 small, meaningful ways to stay on a client's radar—birthday card, moving anniversary, or sharing a resource you know they would value.

- Ask yourself: If I were the client, what kind of follow-up would *make* me feel remembered?

- Create a "Client for Life" checklist. What does great post-close service look like in your business?

- Review your last 3 closings. Did you follow up the way you intended? If not, what's one system you could put in place to help?

- Draft a short check-in script you can use that doesn't sound robotic—just real. Something like: "Hey, I was thinking of you today. How's everything going in the new place?"

- Challenge yourself to follow up with someone this week— not to get business, but to *build a relationship.*

8

The Mindset of a Confident Closer

In my years in real estate, I've closed every deal I've worked on. And in all that time, not one deal has been exactly like another. For a long time, the only thing that felt the same was the paperwork—and even that has changed. Everything else— the homes, the expectations, the personalities, the unexpected issues—was different every single time.

Sometimes, people even became different during the transaction, as stress, excitement, or uncertainty set in along the way. One couple who seemed perfectly aligned at the start found themselves on opposite pages once the negotiations began. Another time, I had to reassure a nervous seller that it wasn't the end of the world just because a buyer backed out. And sometimes, couples become so comfortable with you that they start arguing in front of you — while you politely pretend not to hear a word.

That's why mindset matters so much. Deals can shift quickly, but your ability to keep it all together is what carries you through. And while real estate is an independent business, you're never really alone. You have your managers, other agents, and all the professionals working on the transaction alongside you. That's why teamwork matters—because it's easy to get lost when you try to carry the entire load yourself.

After every transaction, I ask myself:

- Could I have done something better?
- Could I have handled a conversation more clearly?
- Was I present enough for my client?

Confidence doesn't come from being perfect. It comes from showing up consistently and staying coach-able.

One of the greatest sources of confidence in my journey came from my office—particularly my broker and managers.

They're not just experienced—they're seasoned. I'm talking before-computers seasoned. They came up in the business when listings were printed, phones were corded, and relationships were everything.

What stood out most wasn't just their history—it was how consistently they showed up, adapted to the market, and stayed positive—no matter the conditions.

They weren't afraid of change—and they never forgot the fundamentals. They never stopped checking in with us.

"How's business going?" they would ask. I have to admit that sometimes that question made me nervous, but it also lit a fire under me to keep moving. That simple check-in reminded me that success is not just about numbers. It's about awareness. It's about momentum. It's about mindset.

Their longevity and adaptability have shaped me. And now, I carry their example with me every time I speak to a homeowner, meet a buyer, or walk a neighborhood. That's the mindset of a confident closer.

If you want to think like a "Confident Closer", surround yourself with people who already do.

Listen to their stories. Learn from their patience. Let their steadiness strengthen yours.

You don't have to know everything right now. You just have to keep showing up, keep asking better questions, and keep growing—day by day. Confidence isn't a finish line; it's a practice. The more you surround yourself with steady people and keep showing up, the more natural it becomes."

Taking It Further

Confidence isn't loud. It's steady. It's not about having all the answers — it's about knowing where to grow next.

The agents who stay in this business year after year aren't coasting on past wins. They're:

- Checking in.
- Adapting to changes (like the updates in paperwork this past year).
- Leaning on their networks when they need clarity or support.

The Confident Closer isn't just a title — it's a posture built on:

- Self-awareness without self-judgment.
- Progress over perfection.
- A willingness to stay curious, even after years in the field.

Confidence deepens when you do the quiet work: debriefing after a showing, pausing after a phone call, and asking yourself, "What did I learn?" — not just "What did I earn?" It grows when you lean on your team — managers, fellow agents, and the other professionals in the transaction — rather than trying to do everything alone. Independence doesn't mean isolation.

If you want to sharpen your mindset, don't just look ahead — look around:

- Who are you learning from?
- Who speaks into your business — not just your goals, but your growth?
- Who challenges you to be better without making you feel like you're behind?

Those anchors keep you steady when a deal falls through, during slow seasons, and when you miss a monthly or even a year-end goal. They build a confidence that doesn't crack under pressure.

Because the mindset of a Confident Closer isn't built on having all the right moves — it's built on the belief that you'll keep moving, no matter what. Confidence doesn't happen overnight, and it doesn't survive without care. It's something you build through experience, reflection, and the people you surround yourself with.

And even with the right mindset, there's another key to being a Confident Closer — understanding the relationships that drive this business. In real estate, you're not just managing transactions. You're navigating personalities, expectations, and trust. And your mindset determines whether those relationships deepen or crack under pressure.

9

Follow-Up Without Feeling Fake

At one point, the hardest thing for me was the follow-up process.

In real estate, your next opportunity rarely comes from a cold lead. It comes from the way you stay present after the first conversation is over.

Although I was told to do what's called the "drip" process— emails, texts, postcards, and quick online messages—it still felt awkward. Especially when I knew the person wasn't ready to buy or sell or they just weren't ready nor interested.

I would think, *What am I even following up on? They already told me they're not looking.*

They don't know anyone right now. They probably deleted that email, anyway.

But then I realized something that shifted everything: People don't just need an agent when they're ready to buy or sell.

They need someone who helps them stay informed and feel seen—even when there's no transaction on the table.

I had to stop thinking of follow-up as asking for something. And start thinking of it as offering something valuable.

One of the best ways I found to do this was through something I called the "Equity Spotlight." Each report was tailored to their property — not just a generic market sheet anyone could pull online. For homeowners who weren't past clients, I'd sometimes offer the same information as a complimentary gift. Each report was unique to their property, not a generic market sheet. It came naturally to me because it's the kind of thing I would want someone to do for me—help me understand the value of what I own, even when I'm not thinking about selling. And you'd be surprised how often that little gesture sparked conversations I never expected.

Once I let go of the pressure to "convert," my follow-up became more natural.

Instead of thinking, *How do I get a sale out of this?*, I began asking, *What would actually be helpful right now?*

I would send a quick market update—not with a pitch, just information. Or I would forward a listing in their area that matched something we had casually talked about months ago.

Sometimes, I would simply say, "Hey, this reminded me of you. I hope everything's going well." No ask. Just presence. And you know what happened? People started responding.

Not always with, "Let's go see a house," but with gratitude. With curiosity. And occasionally—with a question about rentals, apartments, or someone *they* knew who was kind of...maybe... sort of interested.

And to be completely transparent: my follow-up system hasn't yet produced a closing directly — but it has led to conversations and relationships that later turned into referrals. And some-times, staying in the conversation is the win. It keeps you top of mind. It keeps you connected. It keeps you human.

Taking It Further

Let go of the idea that every follow-up must lead to a sale. The truth is, follow-up is where trust is tested — and trust isn't built in one call or one message.

Follow-up can look like:

- **Sending** one relevant article about the local market.
- **Checking in** during the holidays.
- **Sharing** a resource that could help them long before they're ready to move.

You're not following up to pressure. You're following up to plant seeds. Even if they don't bloom into business right away, they help build your reputation. And in real estate, your reputation moves faster than your marketing.

If your messages feel stale, shift your lens:

- **Ask yourself:** "What would I want someone to send me if I were in their shoes?"
- **Focus on connection, not pitch.** Look for small, genuine ways to stay useful and memorable.

What I know Now

What made follow-up feel better for me was realizing — it's how I want to be treated.

I remember when I took my daughter "college shopping" during her senior year of high school. We went on several tours — some schools she liked, others I knew she probably wouldn't even consider. But the experience was still exciting. It was meaningful. It was hopeful.

There was one college in particular I'll never forget — Hofstra University in New York. She didn't end up enrolling there; she chose another school instead, but the impression Hofstra left on us stayed with me. Four years after she graduated from the college she did choose, a thick Hofstra envelope showed up in our mailbox. She opened it at the kitchen table, surprised to see they were reminding her about graduate school opportunities.

Most colleges send a postcard and disappear. Hofstra reached out four years later. That moved me — not just as a parent, but as a professional. They hadn't forgotten her. They didn't dismiss her "no thank you." They continued to see her as someone with potential.

That one unexpected letter taught me more about follow-up than any sales training I had ever taken.

I want my clients to feel that kind of care—like they matter, even when there's no sale. Like they're seen for who they are, not just what they can do for me today.

That's what real follow-up is. It's not about pestering. It's about presence. It's about treating people the way you hope to be treated — when you're not ready yet, when you're not sure, and even when you've chosen another path.

When you make people feel valued over time, that value comes back to you — often in ways you couldn't predict.

10

When the Fire Fizzles—Just a Little

No one really talks about this part.

When you're doing everything right—you're showing up, you're following up, you're putting yourself out there—and yet, something feels... off.

You're not burned out. You're not giving up. But the excitement has dimmed. That fire you had when you started feels more like a flicker now. It's not gone. It's just not roaring like it used to.

And you start to wonder: *Is something wrong with me?*

Let me tell you something I've learned. That moment? It's normal.

The fire doesn't go out overnight—it just quiets down. And sometimes that quiet happens because other things in your life take priority. It could be personal, professional, financial—or even health related. The fire can also fade a bit when you're juggling too much and wearing too many hats (yours and everyone else). Maybe you're managing family responsibilities, caring for someone you love, handling another job, or trying to keep up with everything all at once. When your attention is pulled in multiple directions, it's natural for your energy toward real estate to shift. That doesn't mean you've lost your passion— it means you're human.

At one point, I felt like I was doing too much, yet not enough. My daughter had needs in college, my full-time job added more responsibilities, and I still had no car. I watched other agents turn sales around quickly while I felt like every moment was starting from scratch. On top of that, I realized I had to be the one to pat myself on the back when those closest to me didn't always understand this journey.

At first, real estate is adrenaline. It's excitement. It's being new and hopeful and full of ideas. But eventually, it becomes rhythm, it becomes strategy, and yes, it becomes a business.

That shift can feel like a letdown, but it's actually a leveling up.

The fire may not feel the same—but now, you're learning how to work with it. You're learning how to keep going when you're not riding the high of a "big win". That's the part that builds longevity.

I've had days where I've questioned everything. I would walk through a neighborhood and see a listing sign that wasn't mine. I would scroll through my inbox and see no leads, no messages, nothing new. I would wonder if people still saw me as a real agent—or just someone "trying."

That's when I made a quiet promise to myself: even on the slow days, I would keep showing up for the small actions like:

- Checking the MLS daily
- Sharing a helpful post
- Sending a thoughtful message to a past client

Not because I felt like it—but because I knew the spark would return. And it always does.

Taking It Further

If you've ever felt on fire one week and stuck the next, you're not alone. Real estate is a people business—but it's also an energy business, and life has a way of pulling on that energy.

The fire doesn't always go out—it can dim under the weight of personal struggles, family duties, health concerns, or money worries. And at times, it flickers simply from carrying more roles than one person should. You can love this business and still have moments where your focus is divided.

Think of it this way: you're building something, even when it feels quiet. Momentum isn't always loud or visible. It's in:

- the way you continue learning
- the way you stay engaged
- the way you follow up with kindness, even when you're not sure where it will lead.

Some of your most meaningful progress will happen behind the scenes—during the quiet weeks, the slow seasons, and the moments when you're deciding whether to rest, reset, or retreat.

Choose to reset. Choose to show up with your name tag on and your mindset open.

And when it all feels like too much, just remember what my broker says:

"Just one."
   -One conversation.
   -One appointment.
   -One piece of business.
   -One closing.
   -One connection that could shift everything.

Some of my best opportunities came from that single small action during the quiet days.

There's no pressure in "just one"—only possibility. That's when real growth happens.

What I Know Now

I've learned to stop chasing that constant "high" of productivity and performance. It's not sustainable. **What *is* sustainable is purpose.** Purpose is what shows up when motivation is taking a break.

And sometimes, it's in those quieter moments—when no one's

calling, when no leads are coming in—that I hear myself more clearly. I remember *why* I started. I remember the people who've trusted me. I remember what it feels like to help someone get to closing day and smile with relief.

That's when the fire comes back. Not as a blaze—but as a steady flame.

I also found that the fire returns when I stay close to the source. For me, that means:

- Staying connected to my team
- Checking in with my broker
- Attending classes—even when I didn't feel like it
- Logging into the MLS regularly
- Learning new tools—(not all of them at once, but enough to grow without feeling overwhelmed)

Sometimes the spark comes from learning something new. Sometimes it comes from hearing a win during a team meeting. Sometimes it comes from simply remembering you're not doing this alone.

The fire may flicker, but it doesn't have to go out. **Stay close to what fuels you**.

11

Focus on What Moves You Forward

As your rhythm starts to take shape, remember—you don't have to master every tool to make an impact. When I first got into real estate, it felt like I stepped into a whole new world. There was so much to learn, and I admired how independent contractors were making real estate happen for so many people. It was inspiring. Every new tool, training, or idea felt like something I wanted to try. I wanted to be involved in everything and know everything. But I quickly realized that as exciting as it was, I was also making it overwhelming for myself.

I had to learn to think smart — focusing on what actually moved my business forward instead of chasing every shiny idea that caught my attention. At one point, I caught myself spending hours on marketing tools and webinars and noticed I wasn't speaking to people the way I should. That realization hit me hard: my energy belonged in conversations, not just information.

There are a lot of moving parts in this business, and sometimes, in trying to "stand out," we start to overthink things. We try to say everything a new way, pitch a new angle, or force ourselves to be clever when what people really need is clarity. There is a big difference between making a script sound like you and constantly rewriting your message. One brings clarity; the other creates confusion.

One of the ways I learned to simplify and focus was by leaning on what already works. In real estate, that often means choosing a few tools you can use well—rather than trying to learn them all. And one of the most valuable tools you can have is a good script. As I mentioned in an earlier chapter, the right script doesn't make you sound fake—it gives your message structure. It helps you stay focused. It helps you communicate clearly in moments when your nerves might want to take over.

You can also practice your rhythm through role-playing with other agents. This may sound awkward at first, but it's one of the fastest ways to build confidence. When I first started, our broker and managers would role-play with the new agents. I stumbled plenty — especially when trying to explain the features and benefits of working with an agent to a "buyer" or "seller."

But that practice mattered. When you rehearse how to respond to common objections or walk through your listing presentation with a peer, you're preparing yourself to stay calm and grounded when it's time to do it for real.

There's a reason athletes run drills. There's a reason singers rehearse. There's a reason public speakers practice in front of the mirror.

Because when the moment comes—you want your body, your mind, and your voice to work together without stumbling. Now, here's the thing—there will always be more you *could* do.

Real estate is full of shiny objects:

- Marketing tools
- Certifications
- Trainings
- Designations
- Social media strategies
- Software systems
- Ads
- Webinars
- AI tools
- Committee meetings
- Social events

Most of these things aren't bad. In fact, some of them are excellent. They can help you grow, connect, and expand what you offer. But if you try to chase them all at once, you'll dilute your time, energy, and impact.

If you're going to get a designation, don't just do it to collect letters behind your name.
Use it. Let it shape the way you serve your clients. Make it part of your real toolkit—not just your email signature. For example, when I earned my SRS and ABR designations, I built a mini-guide for my clients to share the new insights. That one step turned letters after my name into actual value for them.

If you attend committee meetings through your Board of Realtors, be sure you're doing it with intention—not as a way to feel productive while avoiding the work that actually drives your business forward.

The key is focus. You don't need every tool to succeed—you just need the right ones for *your* business. And you'll know you're on the right track when your activities start producing results instead of just filling your calendar.

Focus Plan — From Idea to Practice

This isn't just a tip I read somewhere — it's something I started doing myself and still use when things feel scattered. It's about creating a focus plan and actually putting it into practice.

Try this:

– Jot down three tools, habits, or activities you're using now that actually move your business forward.

– List three "shiny objects" that eat your time without much return.

– Pick one thing you'll double down on this month.

– Pick one thing you'll stop doing or delegate.

Keep this list somewhere you'll see it when you're tempted to "do it all." Focus builds momentum, and momentum builds trust — with your clients and with yourself.

It's easy to get overwhelmed, especially when it feels like there's always something new to learn. Yes, it's important to know your market, stay informed, and sharpen your skills—but don't let the noise distract you from your lane.

Your lane might shift over time. You might start working with investors. Maybe you'll explore commercial properties. Maybe you'll start building relationships in new areas. That's all fine. You're allowed to grow and change. Just don't lose sight of your why—what made you get into this in the first place?

I'll never forget what a former agent once told me. She had moved from another state and said: "To do well in this business, you have to eat, sleep, and dream real estate." And I think she was on to something. This business isn't just about houses. It's about showing up. Staying consistent. Staying prepared. Staying present—even when no one's watching.

There will always be shiny objects in this business. But the agents who last are the ones who know how to keep the main thing the main thing.

The Lesson

Sticking to what works doesn't mean being stuck. It means being steady. It means you're sharpening what you already do well instead of scattering your attention on every new idea that pops up.

Knowing the market is great. Continuing education is important. New designations can open doors. But don't forget the core of it all: relationships, trust, service, and follow-through.

Scripts, routines, and rhythms aren't boring— they're the

backbone of a business built to last. They give you room to focus on people, not just processes.

When you feel pulled in too many directions, remember what my broker always says:
"Just one."

One client. One conversation. One appointment. One day at a time.

Taking It Further

If what you're doing is working, don't second-guess it just because it doesn't look like someone else's approach. You don't have to change your personality or download every new app to keep moving forward.

Refine your process. Know your talking points. Practice with intention. Show up consistently. Follow up with care.

And most of all—protect your focus.

Because when you're locked in on the work that actually matters, you will no longer need to chase "shiny objects" but will start building something that lasts.

12

Keep Doing

I must admit, writing this book was therapeutic for me — not because I ever felt like giving up, but because I did feel like slowing down.

Sometimes, it's not burnout — it's just being full:

- Full of advice.
- Full of pressure.
- Full of thoughts about what you should be doing.

You know you have something to give, but people are busy. You try to show up, you try to stay consistent, and it can be tough when others don't respond with the same energy you're putting out.

Tomorrow Is Your Reset Button

Here's one thing I've learned: not everyone will be as excited about your business as you are. And that's okay. Because you are the one who must stay excited. You are the one who sees the vision, and sometimes you're the only one clapping for yourself. But then—there's tomorrow.

Tomorrow is such a strong word:

- It's a reason to get up again.
- It's a pause and a reset button.
- It tells you, "Try again."

It doesn't have to come with guarantees, but it does come with possibilities.

You may have had a deal fall through. You may have walked past a property in your own neighborhood with another agent's sign on the lawn and felt that gut punch. We've all been there.

But tomorrow reminds you: this isn't over. This is just one day in a career full of them. When setbacks come, don't panic—pivot:

- Reset your focus.
- Reconnect with your network.
- Relearn the basics that build confidence.

It is your opportunity to show up again.

This business moves fast, but tomorrow always slows things

down to what you can do—today. You don't have to conquer the market in one week. Just keep doing the work. And the work will eventually work for you.

Stay In It

You've seen the highs, the dips, the awkward moments, and maybe a few big wins. You're not here by accident. And even if the results haven't shown up yet the way you imagined them— you're still becoming the agent you were meant to be.

Just don't stop. You're building a career that's layered in real connections, not just transactions. And that means showing up even when it's not glamorous. Following up even when you think it won't matter. Being present in a world full of shortcuts and bots.

The Heart Behind the Work

We live in a time of quick answers, text responses, and all things AI—but people still need people.

- There's no app that can replace a sincere conversation or a supportive ear when a client's offer gets rejected for the fifth time.
- There's no AI-generated message that matches the feeling of handing someone the keys to their new home.

So, What Do We Do? We Keep Doing.

Here are some of the simple, consistent habits that keep me moving forward:

- **We keep reaching out to prospects** — because sometimes people just need a reminder that someone cares.
- **We keep up with the market** — so we can break it down in a way that helps our clients make confident decisions.
- **We keep in touch with our past clients** — because the relationship doesn't end at the closing table.
- **We keep paying the dues** — literally and figuratively.
- **We keep guiding the transaction** — holding it together through inspection hiccups, financing delays, and last-minute negotiations.
- **We keep learning.**
- **We keep showing up.**
- **We keep growing.**

Because this is more than a job. It's a journey. And no matter how long it takes or how hard it gets—**We. Keep. Doing.**

My broker always says, "This is a doing class." And honestly, that's what this business is.

- Not a waiting business.
- Not a watching business.
- A doing business.

So go ahead. Close with confidence — and keep doing what you were called to do.

Self-Check

Before you move on, take a few quiet minutes to reflect on what you've read so far. Use these prompts to focus your energy and plan your next steps:

- What's one small action you can take tomorrow to move your business forward, even if you don't feel motivated?
- Where do you find yourself chasing "shiny objects" instead of focusing on conversations?
- Who is one past client, neighbor, or lead you could reach out to this week just to check in?
- What energizes you most about real estate right now? How can you build more of that into your week?
- When was the last time you felt the "spark"? What were you doing that day?
- What part of your business do you need to "reset" instead of "retreat"?

13

Questions That Build Trust

Once you've taken that first step and made the initial connection, the real challenge is keeping the conversation flowing naturally. Good questions aren't just about getting answers—they spark dialogue, show you're listening, and give the other person a reason to keep hearing from you.

Questions That Show Care in Action

These are some of the questions that I have used over the years. They're not magic scripts — just gentle ways of keeping a conversation going and letting people know I'm thinking about them. Use whichever phrasing feels natural to you.

- **"What have you noticed about the market in your neighborhood lately?"**
- *(Another way: "What have you been hearing about what homes like yours are selling for?")*
- **"What kinds of homes or features are you most drawn to**

when you're browsing online or driving around?"
- *(Or: "What's the last home you saw that made you think, 'That's interesting'?")*
- **"When you picture your next home, what's something you would love to have that you don't have now?"**
- *(Or: "What feature would make you feel, 'This is the one'?")*
- **"What has your experience been so far with buying or selling? What worked and what didn't?"**
- *(Or: "What stood out about the last agent you worked with?")*
- **"Which neighborhoods have you been curious about exploring?"**
- *(Or: "If you could get the inside scoop on one area, which one would you pick first?")*
- **"What would help you feel most prepared for your next move?"**
- *(Or: "What would make the process feel less stressful for you?")*
- **"As you think about your next move, how are you weighing location, style, and price?"**
- *(Or: "If you had to choose, which matters most right now — location or type of home?")*
- **"What kind of market updates would be most useful for you?"**
- *(Or: "When information changes, how do you prefer to hear about it?")*
- **"What's your ideal timeline if you decide to make a move?"**
- *(Or: "When would moving feel right for you?")*
- **"What do you love most about your current home that you would want to keep in the next one?"**
- *(Or: "What's the one thing you would hate to give up?")*
- **"What would you like to know about getting your home ready to sell, even if it's down the road?"**

- *(Or: "Would a short checklist on show-ready tips be useful?")*
- **"What's changed for you since we last spoke about your housing plans?"**
- *(Or: "How can I adjust what I'm sending you based on your current situation?")*

The Care-First Formula

Reading about lawsuits and changing brokerage rules has been a wake-up call for me as an agent. They are proof that when clients feel unseen, the entire profession feels it. Rather than seeing that as discouraging, I see it as a chance to lead differently. The Care-First Formula is my daily reminder to build trust, give clear guidance, and protect the reputation of our business one conversation at a time.

Over the years I began to notice a pattern: the agents who keep clients informed, who anticipate questions before they're asked, who educate instead of just sell, and who listen instead of tell are the ones who build careers that last. That's the spirit behind my Care-First Formula.

Here's how I keep it at the heart of my business:

C – Connect with Intention

Don't just "check in"—*connect.* Ask about their family, their pets, their latest vacation. Remember birthdays, moving anniversaries, and milestones. Whether it's a phone call, text, or handwritten card, make it personal.

A – Anticipate Needs

Your clients shouldn't have to wonder what's next—you should be two steps ahead. From prepping them for inspections to giving them a heads-up about closing costs, anticipating needs makes the process feel easier and less stressful.

R – Respond Quickly

Timely communication builds trust. Even if you don't have an answer yet, a quick "I'm on it and will update you soon" tells them they matter. In a competitive market, speed isn't just nice—it's necessary.

E – Educate at Every Step

Clients can't make confident decisions if they don't understand the process. Explain terms, walk them through contracts, and translate market data into plain language. Education is empowerment—and empowered clients refer you.

Mindset Before Marketing

It is tempting to think success starts with the right postcard design, social media post, or clever slogan. But your mindset is the real foundation. Marketing gets people's attention. Your mindset keeps their trust.

A Care-First mindset means you:

- show up even when the phone is quiet;
- serve clients with the same effort whether it is a $200k condo or a $2M estate;

- measure success not only in sales but in trust earned and relationships built.

Why the Care-First Formula Works

People remember how you made them feel long after they forget the details of the transaction. By focusing on care first, you:

- stand out in a crowded market;
- build a network of loyal clients and referral partners;
- protect your business from market ups and downs — because relationships built with care can outlast a single transaction or market cycle.

Markets change. Technology changes. Strategies change. But care never goes out of style. The Care-First Formula is not a "nice extra." I believe it is the core of a business that lasts.

14

Bonus: More Questions That Build Trust

These are conversation starters I've used to get past small talk and into helpful, human dialogue. You don't need to ask them all. Pick one or two that fit naturally with the flow of your conversation, then let the dialogue do the rest. And remember to build toward the most important question of all: **asking for the business**. As my broker says, "Always build up to the appointment." Sometimes that's as simple as, Do you need my help? Because I'm available.

When I'm speaking with a homeowner who's thinking about selling, these are the kinds of questions I might ask to understand their real goals and concerns.

Questions for Sellers

1. What's leading you to think about selling right now?
2. Where do you see yourself next—staying nearby or going somewhere new?
3. What's the main reason for the move—finances, lifestyle,

or something else?

4. When you picture this move going smoothly, What matters the most to you— speed, price, or convenience?

5. Have you sold a home before? What was that experience like?

6. What's your vision for the next chapter in your life—when would you like it to start?

7. When you imagine closing day, what would make it feel like a win for you?

8. Have you already picked your next home—or are you still exploring?

9. What, if anything, worries you about putting your home on the market?

10. Have you thought about any repairs for or updates before listing, would you like me to take a look and give some input?

11. Would you like me to arrange to have your home professionally photographed?

12. How do you feel about open houses versus private showings?

13. Would it be helpful If I shared what homes nearby are selling for right now?

14. I'm curious—have you already chatted with any other agents about your plans?

15. What part of this next chapter are you looking forward to the most?

16. What do you think will be the toughest part about saying goodbye to this home?

17. Are there any memories or little things about the house you would love the next owner to appreciate?

18. As we go through this together, what would help you feel

most supported?

When I'm meeting with a buyer or a potential buyer, I use these questions to uncover what matters most to them and how I can guide them through the process.

Questions for Buyers

1. What sparked your decision to start looking for a home right now?
2. Please share with me what your dream home is like?
3. Which features feel like must-haves, and which would simply be nice bonuses?
4. If everything lined up perfectly, when would you like to move in to your new home?
5. Have you had a chance to connect with a mortgage representative yet?
6. How does commuting fit into you plans—is there a distance you are comfortable with?
7. Do you see your next home as a stepping stone for a few years?
8. Do you imagine hosting gatherings or do you prefer quiet settings?
9. How important are schools, walk ability, or neighborhood features to you?
10. Do you prefer move-in ready—or are you open to something that needs a little work?
11. What monthly payment range feels comfortable to you?
12. Are there any financial deal-breakers that I should know about?

13. How do you feel about bidding wars or multiple-offer situations?
14. Have you bought a home before? What was that experience like—and what would you change this time?
15. What's been the hardest part of your search so far?
16. Have you seen anything you liked but didn't move on? Why?
17. What's your biggest concern about the process?
18. Who else will be involved in making the decision?
19. What's one thing you wish someone would explain about buying a home?
20. What does "home" mean to you?
21. If I found you the perfect home tomorrow, what would it include?
22. Are you drawn to any particular style—modern, traditional, historic?
23. What kind of feeling do you want the home to have when you walk in the door?
24. What do you picture doing your first weekend in your new home?
25. How would you prefer me to communicate with you—text, email, phone?
26. When you think "great agent" what should stand out to you?
27. What's something you've appreciated (or not appreciated) from past agents?
28. How involved do you want to be in the search and offer process?
29. What would help you feel completely confident about moving forward?
30. Are you curious as to how agents actually get paid?

Most of the time, people just want to be in the know — and that's okay. The key is helping them reflect on *why* they're interested in the first place. When home-ownership or the housing market comes up, make sure the person walks away not only with good information but also with a question answered and maybe a new question to think about.

Sometimes people aren't ready to move yet — they're just curious. These questions help me keep the conversation light but meaningful.

Conversation Starters for the "Just Curious" Crowd

1. Have you been thinking about buying a home, or is renting still working for now?
2. If the perfect place came along—right price, right location—would you consider it?
3. What makes you curious about the market, as oppose to actively moving?
4. When people talk about the market, what are you hoping to learn?
5. Have you explored what homes are going for in the area you like?
6. Have you ever stopped by an open house just to look around?
7. What would need to fall into place for you to consider buying?
8. Would it be helpful if I showed you what's really happening in your neighborhood—not the headlines, but actual listings?

9. Have you ever spoken to a lender just to see what's possible?
10. What's the biggest question you'd want answered before starting?
11. Do you know the first step if you decided to explore buying?
12. Have you ever wondered how your rent compares to what a mortgage might cost?
13. If you were approved today, would you know where to start looking?
14. Would you like to see what's possible in your price range—just out of curiosity?
15. Are you thinking short-term stay, or putting down roots?
16. If timing, money, and credit weren't an issue, what would your ideal home look like?
17. Have you noticed friends or coworkers buying lately? Did it get you thinking?
18. Would you say you're "just looking," or looking for a plan?
19. What would make you feel more confident about home-ownership—information, a guide, or just someone to talk it through?
20. You don't have to be ready to buy to ask questions. Do you want me to provide you a quick breakdown of how the process works?
21. Do you need assistance looking into home-ownership, because I am available?

Keep in mind that these question are based on conversations that you are having with people who are homeowners and property owners or future buyers. Just think, if you were at a backyard gathering and conversations about the market and home ownership come up, these are the questions that you may want to ask or these might be already in the conversation.

You don't need to turn casual conversation into an information session. Instead, keep your ears open and make sure people are getting accurate information. You can even ask, "Where did you hear that?" and gently clarify what's true.

Now, you may come across some people who believe that they know enough about the market to not want to engage in a conversation with you, the agent. But, we still want to know how the consumer thinks about the housing market. I would then ask that person questions and let them know that it is important for agents to know what consumers think about what they've heard regarding the market or about real estate in general. You can pivot the conversation to, What do you think about the prices of homes nowadays? How do you feel about it? What do you think the pros and cons of selling or buying in today's market?

With homeowners who are simply watching the market or wondering about their options, these questions open a friendly door without pressure.

Conversation Starters for Curious Homeowners

1. What's been the biggest change you've noticed in your neighborhood over the past few years?
2. If someone new moved in next door, what would you tell them you love most about living here?

3. When you first bought this home, what made you think, "Yes, this is the one"?
4. Has anything about the market lately caught your attention — prices, interest rates, or new listings?
5. If a neighbor's house sold tomorrow, what would you be most curious about — the price, the buyer, or the timing?
6. Have you ever stopped by a neighbor's open house to see what's on the market?
7. If life circumstances changed and you needed to move, what kind of place would you picture yourself in next?
8. What kind of updates or changes have you made that you're most proud of?
9. Do you see this as your long-term home, or more of a stepping stone to something else?
10. Would it be helpful if I gave you a simple snapshot of what homes like yours are actually selling for — no pressure, just information?
11. When you hear news about the housing market, what's the first question that pops into your head?
12. If someone offered to do a quick home-equity check for you, would you find that interesting?

And when coming across a For-Sale-By-Owner, don't jump into a pitch. Start with respectful, low-pressure questions like these to build rapport and offer value. These are not meant to corner someone. They are meant to **start a respectful conversation** with homeowners who've chosen to go it alone.

Questions for FSBO (For-Sale-By-Owner) Sellers

1. I noticed your sign and also saw the home online. I know you have probably had a lot of calls already, but would you mind if I came by to see the property?
2. What do you love most about this home that you hope the next buyer will notice?
3. Are you handling all the showings yourself, or do you prefer to schedule certain times?
4. What kind of response have you gotten so far — more calls, showings, or just people driving by?
5. If a buyer asked me about your neighborhood, what's something you would want me to tell them?
6. Have you run into any surprises in the process, or has it gone mostly how you expected?
7. If the right buyer came along tomorrow, do you already have an attorney or title company lined up?
8. Would it be helpful if I kept you in mind if I meet a buyer who is looking for a home like yours?
9. What's been the most time-consuming part of selling on your own so far? Do you need assistance because I am available?
10. If I came across a buyer who seemed like a fit, would you want me to let you know or wait until you reach out?

There are probably more questions that you may have or you may just change these entirely, it's up to you. It is more about connecting and staying in touch. When we ask questions with care, curiosity, and respect, they become bridges that build trust.

Afterword

Before You Close This Book

You made it to the end—but this is far from over. You didn't pick up this book because you're unsure of who you are.

You picked it up because something in you knows you're built for more. You've learned to listen differently.

- To ask better questions.
- To walk into conversations with care, not pressure.
- To show up—whether it's your first year or your fifteenth.

You've been reminded that confidence:

- Isn't loud.
- It's not scripted.
- It's definitely not perfect.
- It's in the quiet follow-ups.
- The honest answers.
- The steady showing up—even when no one's clapping yet.

I'm still learning these things too. Writing this book has been part of my own growth — sorting through what's worked, what hasn't, and how to keep moving forward.

So before you close this book, maybe ask yourself (the same way I ask myself):

- What's one conversation I've been putting off that I can have this week?
- Who's one client I can follow up with, just to check in?
- What would the most confident version of me do next?

Whatever your answer is—start there. And then, keep going. Because you're not just a reader of this book. You're a doer.

And I'm right here on the journey with you — just a few steps ahead, still practicing what I've written.

This book isn't the end. It's a place to begin again.

www.ingramcontent.com/pod-product-compliance
Lightning Source LLC
Chambersburg PA
CBHW040907210326
41597CB00029B/5005